You're Going to Miss Me When You're Bored

You're Going to Miss Me When You're Bored

Justin Marks

Barrelhouse Books
Baltimore, Maryland
www.barrelhousemag.com

Cover by M. Joshua Elliott
Interior designed by Justin Sirois

Library of Congress Cataloging-in-Publication Data:
Marks, Justin
You're Going to Miss Me When You're Bored/Justin Marks
Library of Congress Control Number: 2014901547

First Edition, 2014
ISBN: 978-0-9889945-1-5
Printed in the United States of America

Acknowledgements

Many thanks to the editors of the following journals in which these poems appeared:

Agricultural Reader, Barrelhouse, Denver Quarterly, Failbetter, Free Verse, Harp & Altar, Horse Less Review, Interrupture, Leveler, LIT, Octopus, Similar : Peaks, Sink Review, Sixth Finch, So and So Broadsides, Tusculum Review.

Many thanks to the editors who published chapbooks in which many of these poems appeared: Rope-a-Dope (*Voir Dire*), Poor Claudia (*On Happier Lawns*) and Dikembe Press (*We Used to Have Parties*).

Thanks to Ana Božičević and Željko Mitić for translating poems from this book into Serbian and including them in *The Day Lady Gaga Died: an Anthology of NYC Poetry of the 21st Century (in Serbian, Peti talas/The Fifth Wave, 2011).*

Thanks to Dan Boehl, Julia Cohen, Shanna Compton, Jennifer L. Knox, Keith Newton, Matt Rasmussen, Sampson Starkweather and Chris Tonelli for their time, patience, care, inspiration and keen editorial eyes.

Thanks to Josh Elliott for the cover design and Justin Sirois for the interior layout.

Thanks to Melissa Broder, Wayne Coyne and Daniel Handler for the kind words.

Thanks to my editor, Dan Brady, and everyone at Barrelhouse.

Thanks to Meridith Rohana, above all, for endless love and support, and to Henry and Louisa Marks—the best people on the planet.

Contents

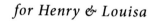

for Henry & Louisa

VOIR DIRE

I live in New York City and a horse
goes clopping by my window.
Then I don't
hear the horse anymore.
All promises
have been broken.
I lie in bed and pretend
to sleep. On occasion
I see babies sleeping,
little ones lying
on their backs
with baby bones
and skeletons
and organs that function.
They see and hear
and taste and smell.
They learn to speak and feel
awkwardness and shame.
It's good that we don't
remember being babies.
It's good to feel good.
Sometimes I fall
for things I shouldn't.
I think of my parents
with a kind
of regret and sympathy
for us all. A process,
like anything else.
A series of questions
raised in silence.
It's an adventure
inside my body right now,
not knowing what will happen.
Something gets forced in,
returns out.
Whatever it is,
I say it alone,

aloud. I decide
on a course of thought
or action, and inevitably
wind up pursuing the other.
I'm happy
to be indignant,
but also just happy.
I share a pizza
and movie with my wife.
She is like a carrot
and I'm a little rabbit.
Our babies will be orange.
A bug is pressed
into a book's pages
on the shelf.
Tourists get their pictures taken
in front of great works of art.
A young couple French
-kisses outside
the Museum of Sex.
The moon is full and shining
magnificently over
the rivers, Hudson and East.
I'm 6 feet tall and tone deaf,
a truly terrible singer.
I've always been swayed
by the belief that the maker
should not be able to see
himself in his art. I see
nothing but myself.
Plastic flowers in a lush,
green garden on
the Lower East Side, Avenue C.
Pinocchio standing before
a table of wood-working tools.
I know you know
I'm spying on you

spying on me
spying on you. That's
what makes this fun,
right? Penetrate to
the most high god
and you'll go insane,
I hear. Even
the speed of light
isn't fast enough
to save you.
But don't be afraid.
It's only the pressure
that's difficult to bear.
Amusement park rides,
even children's corkscrew
playground slides
make me nauseous.
Mothers yell at their children
and their children cry.
The limits of my linear mind.
I sometimes believe everything
I'll ever do or say
is already inside
someone else.
What *was* I thinking
when I marked that passage
in the book that read,
This is older than towns?
As a child, my favorite
part of the day was coming home
and getting the mail,
wondering what,
if anything, was addressed
to me. I wish sleep
was a switch I could simply throw.
Sobriety and intoxication as well.
The immense joy I receive

when reading my sent emails.
Also in finally getting straight
the spellings of *decent*
and *descent*.
All day at the beach,
children stomp
out of the surf and onto
the shore. New organisms,
in the grand scheme of things.
My back is terribly sun-burnt.
Peeling. I get chills and forget
everything I've learned.
I'm a Mayflower
descendent. My great
-great grandfather
was a Russian-Jewish immigrant.
Riding in a cab
up the West Side Highway,
a little tipsy,
the salt-water air
and boat fumes...
I get incredibly inspired,
but not for long.
A bowl of fresh
blueberries and glass
after glass of water
await my arrival
home.
A hard-boiled
egg for breakfast.
The cat. My wife.
The future generation
we have yet to have.
Where did this weight
I've gained come from?
Why can't I lose it?
I'm in my early-thirties,

my grandparents are dead
and my parents are old.
Frequent déjà vu
renders everything inevitable.
When my wife comes home
she will kiss me and remove
her clothes, stretch out
across the bed and we will
discuss the day. Most
of my good fortune
is a fluke.
The bad as well.
That's as far
as it ever seems to go.
Another flabby body
at the gym
trying to look good,
a relation relating itself
to itself.
There are no answers,
only variations
in understanding.
Which is the purpose
of speech. Words.
Again and again.
It's to myself I mostly talk.
A man walking past
me on the subway platform chants,
Christmas, Christmas, Christmas.
On a large envelope I drop
in the mail I write repeatedly,
Do Not Bend.
Discovery of one thing
by way of another.
The material of the cosmos crumpling
until all possible paths
narrow to one.

I'm completely addicted
to my email. Can't go without
checking it every few minutes.
Connection to the outside
world via the virtual.
Things either occur
or they don't.
The lavender my mother helped
my wife transplant is dying.
One of the more satisfactory
experiences of my life
was moshing so hard
I broke my retainer.
Twenty-three years ago.
There are no
discreet events. History
is in everything.
And memory. Dim
notions coming into focus,
then fading.
In a different life
I'd like to have been
a B-movie star.
Napping on the couch I tell
myself I'm not sleeping at all, just
relaxing, absorbing
the sound of traffic,
the sun and air
through the open window.
Putting a little spring
back in my step.
All this love
and hatred in my heart.
But if I could just stay awake,
if I could just stay awake long enough
it might all work out. This day
barely begun.

On Happier Lawns

I

In the days of yore I was a parakeet and my mouth
a river   The lights low to see
into other worlds   Vessels completing
circuits   Ancient conjurings and obscure
geometries   Screens so lovely
If I have a true self it is you   Blood, slow
Dimensionally agnostic and lost in the loam   A gun-
powder portrait or arc that ends with smashing
into glass   Skeletons scanned   An imaged sky
If you hold me in your head I will be happy
An edible ghost   Encoded identity in a cloud
of processors   The difference you experience entirely
different   Perforated form   Sad
appendage   The heart, a stencil

II

A disordered army and someone
going on about ontological bowling
and the onomatopoeia
of the people praying
for their pins to drop
The past and all its bad
haircuts   Buildings speak
of the horizon
and its electro-folk
atmosphere
My head pounding
and guitar solos filled
with elaborate promises   Crush
or chew or swallow whole

III

I love being drunk   Then I don't
I love drinking   A summoning
I look at the women and the women
look scared   The days of Hollywood are over
and these cinders are all that's left
of the evening's meal   A feast   A candy
store in my brain   The historical and personal
significance of intercourse
I believe in saving myself
for marriage   A number to call
like a breast to suckle   My past
riddled with ignorance and delusion
A jugular vein leaking
the most interesting colors

IV

The bizarre sound of my own
name repeating and people
praying
My hair getting
unwieldy in a world filled
with an abundance that approaches
formlessness   Strangeness
and beauty   Truth
is a melody like a leach
or the aftermath of the disaster
there is no trace of   A killer
sunset
When you open your eyes
someone familiar may be waiting

V

Love endures like war
A connection I make then let
be unmade   Some guy
nodding out in a Starbucks,
severe career advice
from strangers   It's 1pm and reality
is palpable   A gun
I leave my DNA wherever I can
and have no opinions to speak of
except when showering
When I was 8 my mother threw
a drink in my face   A taste
of blood   The clouds were a show
all on their own

VI

Not everything I'm telling you
will be true   Rudeness   People
disappearing   Seamless
messages to readers on separate
computer screens
Colorful curtains
throwing pale shadows
Some people believe tourism is the key
to peace   Men who mean business
Disordered armies pulling each other on
to victory   A child
who comes up to you and says,
I was alive for five years

VII

A pill the first thing
every morning   Behind the eyes
where the view is broadcast
water towers and cranes
Sunlight   Winter
It's dead outside but alive
in here   Concepts and forms   Intros
and endings   Memory
is merely a mock-up   A creepy
little doll   At age 32
I had my first wet-dream   My inner
strength is my money   A mild
discomfort   Something making me sad
but I don't know what

VIII

Dreaming in the driver's seat
with an acute fear
of buttoning my jacket   The rest
on the cutting room floor
Just say what to do and it will be
summer   Wondrous
Soft and fuzzy   I don't mean
to make no fuss
Truth is a traffic accident
in which bones break
the skin   Procrastination
in a foreign language
Betrayal of one's best instincts
I saw a femur once

IX

Toothpicks from a dead man's
estate   A baby
crying through a bull-horn
I project myself into the future
as a slogan on a sandwich
board   Tennis at 3   Homemade
sex tapes   I'm so happy
I could puke   I'm typing so hard
it feels like I chipped
some bones in my fingers
At night, wine and Xanax
Bursts and inconsistency
A messaging system that transfers
the self composing the words

X

Jack Spicer on my iPod
A beach   Whatever language it is
the ocean makes   It's New Year's
and waves are passing
It's New Year's   Mute animals
are singing   An island   Distance
Somewhere a child's
first word is *uterus*   The surf
is rough   An agnostic audience
The brine in my beard
is a sliver of meaning
The dancing bear   A mosquito
feeding   The ant I'm about
to flick from my foot

XI

Reckless of hand, a trembling knife
Collaborative regrets   I'm all juiced up on something
but can't tell what   O memory
have I got plans for you
I'm so off-key I can feel my lips
buzz when I sing   The streets reek of smoked
weed   A thousand fires   A language
speaking for itself   The IT
technician is the ghost in my computer
A brilliant disguise   Cancelled innovation
or childhood that simply
will not die   A real downer but I'm not
one to reminisce
You're going to miss me when you're bored

XII

The ring is a hole I slide
my finger through
A loop of flukes and fortunes
like a mimetic goddamn
or the city over time
in which truth is buried   Beauty
its demolition   Speaking
is an actuality
Silence too   Revelations
and attendant regrets in which
the self is a copy to sell   The concept
and the form
A bladder completely emptied
into a beautiful urinal

XIII

A forced smile
may or may not reveal
teeth   A destination   I could be convinced
of basically anything
The public has a power all its own
A knack for causing disarray
as symbolized by my hair   Affection
distracts from loneliness
How many times was it we fucked
The beach   The bed   The national
wildlife refuge   Overcome
by sadness   Kind of perfect
A girl in a tiara collecting shells
I try not to get involved

XIV

A hand dents the universe in the dark
interior of my pants pocket
A bit of theater   Aesthetic outbursts
to speed up truth and
attendant beauty   Dreams folded endlessly
and the result is damaged
bones   An accident of the mouth passed off
as love   Coldness mitigated by the sun
Pretty   Very pretty   The work
that will never be done   The anatomy
of a page that is primarily
redaction   A genuine(ly disappointing)
personality   If ever we meet
on happier lawns

XV

Mediocrity mounts
its attempts at more   Weapons I
download to my phone
Less air and water than hope
and memory   You rivers   You waterfalls
You ribs of broken pencils
The difficulty of being a "person"
is "sincerity"   And other
protocols   Fingernails
on fire   The truth
bores me   My
amphetamine soul
You'd be better off
staying at home

XVI

Overwrite your memory too many
times and you start
to hear old voices   The ominous
clacking of computer keys   Awareness
as a function of interaction   My arsenal
is icicles   Pinch point hazards
and disconnect panels   A curse
that rots the mouth   I have
begun to hear old voices   Bullets
defiled by words and their
attendant fluids   The past and all its
crashed cars   Clear paths
to completion   A sky gone wrong
The sun cracked open

XVII

O my literal mind   It can only handle
so much   The menstruating sky
It's empty womb   The facts that do not do
what I want them to   It's important
to stay aware of the pain   That brand
of invention   The mostly embarrassing
past   To no longer care
about winning   That ever
fading figure   It's frigid shores
The malady is the melody   No subject
No sender   A self awaiting
further destruction   Exhilarating
fear   Insert
dead people here

XVIII

Sometimes saying things helps
me see them   The memory
of a sacred so and so   Commands
written into the code   My hair
is a joke   *There was an error*
creating the error message,
says the computer   *We will win*
and publish our enemies,
says a friend   A book and a gun
prefaced by love   It's 9am and already
I'm thinking about lunch   White noise
rumbling in my loins   The end
of brilliance and fame   A reinvented
kiss   Magnificent decomposition

XIX

I shake a notebook of empty
pages and say, *It's all in here*
Every word of it   Dead dogs and stolen
property   Embraced
debauchery   For 35 years I had
no story to tell   Only words
in need of form   Every breath
a bomb   An infinite
space to fill   I see now that death
is just an idea   A very real
idea   As much an ethos as
aesthetic   Textured
sadness   Language etched
into fiber optics   Which is to say, light

NAÏVE MELODY

I want to write a poem where I drop all pretense and simply talk
as straightforward as I can.

Of course, that requires huge assumptions on my part.
For example, who are you?

I drive a minivan and my beard   is graying.

When I was five I was almost hit by a truck while crossing
the street on my bike

but something told me to keep pedaling, hard,
a voice, I guess,
        though it sounded an awful lot
                like mine.

Which almost makes me believe something or someone is
looking out for me. Or was.

        Most of my friends
                are getting divorced.

My cat wakes me every morning at 4 by hooking her claw into
my nostril to let me know she wants to eat.

Religious and spiritual people say that reality is just an illusion
and I can get with that, but who's to say there's anything better.

        The poverty of poetry.
                The language of language.

No no no, says my daughter.   *Yes yes yes*, says her mother.

        (Strange to call my wife her mother.)

A poet-critic I admire says,
*You have to read everybody. And that's a horrible burden, so just
read what you want to read. But how do you know what you
want to read? How do you know?*

I recently read an article about a poet who fell madly in love
only to have her heart broken. *I dedicated my whole life to
literature, she said. My whole life to poetry. I didn't know what
love was. If I had known, if I had known earlier, I wouldn't have
dedicated my life to literature. I would have dedicated it to love.*

Eventually, she killed herself.

What I'm trying to say is, it's difficult, all this uncertainty,
exhausting, really, each moment being consumed
by trying always to make the right decision—

not think about

the ways

I've failed.

Pink Clouds of the Apocalypse

*

The assassin is loose
I'm drinking a Diet Dr. Pepper
Your boyfriend wants to punch me in the face
for the sex I had with you
in a dream   Things are
as they are(n't)   An impending
release   A crevice in my foot   The twin streams
of my pee   Links
to whatever   I just put on some bug repellant and it really
seems to be working   I feel so
quasi-apocalyptic   Progress at this point
is a myth   A record of words   I trust completely
in corporate media   The end
of the end   A brand new century
When I think about my wife and children I wonder,
how did that happen   It's all
so overwhelming   Not seeing what's here
for amazement that it exists
Conflict, inevitable   An endorsement deal   A peal
of laughter   Nature itself is a conspiracy
theory   An inhabitance   The presentation
that never ends   The difference between
morning and night is wine   Sometimes I get
incapacitated   If I can't imagine an outcome
I assume it means I won't live to see it   Old age
My children grown

That was the frequency and this is something
I had a feeling for   I'm envious
of your hair   Its proliferation   Language
Its accusations   I hold a knife and feel like
using it   *This message has no content,*
says an email that didn't download to my phone
Help is on the way, says a button in an elevator
My fingernails keep growing   The ceiling
looks like a cantaloupe rind
But I love walking around like this
An open mess   A look like maybe
I hate life   The proud purchaser
of a new home

*

Innumerable people of creative talent
I must express my joy   The message of days
is a disconnected tongue   Awkward stains
and beer bottles on baby teeth   Dynamic
data in a pinch   Interruption
is the rhythm   An operational (w)hole   Absence
as visibility is the value   Equal disappointment   A happy
marriage   The enemy
is an anemone   I'll never be a rock star
but that's not going to stop me
from coming up with names for bands—
Pond Snail Meth-Head   The Thousandaires
What's Your Major?
I hide my prurience in civility   Discard my lanyard
and I'm lost   The silence
is excitement   A timid little teether all wrapped up
in reverb   Bio-luminescent creatures shining
in a bay on a night of low
light pollution   The colors of dawn—hysterical—travel along
my bones   An average beauty   A sales force charging
into the night

*

It's summer and sex
is everywhere
My greatest motivation
is fear of my children
dying   *I'm a body*, says my daughter
Your body   When my back aches
my shoulder itches
The key to marriage,
I profess to my single friends,
is not getting divorced
My son yells from his bed,
daddy, daddy, daddy,
then a bunch of sounds
I don't understand
Rooster in a rocket   Snail on Saturn
Fist-fights and vices intervening
Dudes with guitars
My life is 1.5 times more complicated
than many, but not as much
as others   My wife
faints   My daughter loses
her breath   My son
sleeps through it all

*

The poem is a problem
only a fool would want to solve   Ridiculous
music   A meaningless
tattoo   Burn blisters that resemble
redactions   Silence that leads
to shipwreck   Such
exaggerated laughter   At work
I listen to really bad indie-rock
and washed up glam bands
A mentally ill man
kicks me in the shin   Dead mice
and screaming babies   Everyone looks
so unencumbered
All you can make clear
is complexity
is a conclusion I often come to
A real metafucker

*

It's hot   My back hurts   My soul
is floating   I go to sleep in one place
and wake up in another   The inner workings
of a remarkable thing   A fine lie
It's like I'm in everyone's living room,
says a man next to me on the subway
I'm probably lying,
says a t-shirt hanging in a store window.
To all my ex-girlfriends I just want to say, *isn't it weird*
we ever fucked   What I mean is
what the words mean
Inappropriate touches and silly
sentimentality   Pink clouds
of the apocalypse   A battened down light   Night-night
on the night-night

Interruption Is the Rhythm

A BIT OF DREAMING

I have an appetite for glass,
a diamond necklace that needs fixing.
My ex-fiancé is pregnant and I'm
still trying to sleep with her.
We drink some beers. Sidenote:
last time I dreamt someone was pregnant
they were pregnant.
A bag of lines biding its time.
A ship of thoughts.
The fluid mechanics of a cat's tongue
lapping liquid is the command:
Sacrifice until there's nothing left.
There's always something left.
Itches itching.
Chicken that tastes like shrimp.
Batteries on bones. Also please note:
The laser through the diamond that destroys
the earth was my most diabolical plot.
My son falls from a great height
and I wake up crying.
Then not. Often, I get shot.
When a woman standing on the corner
breastfeeding a baby strapped to her chest
holds out a hat, we all contribute.
The baby moves its head
to reveal the mother's breast.
Then something happens
involving a surfboard. A juicy goose.
Dresses drawing eyes to all the wrong

places. New water on naked stems. The sex
is unreal. A missile launch
or geyser erupting, dirty bombs
that explode. A yellow-faced
Walt Whitman holds his hat and stares
at a plaque with his birth
and death dates on it.
I take a workshop in which the teacher
assigns poets so obscure
they have emoticons for names,
impossible to Google.
A prayer for truth. Viscous attack. My brain
bleeds eyes. I pack a bowl
full of pasta. Welcome punches
to my paunchy belly.
Chuck some pumpkins down on the farm.
Most of what I say
is what I need. On amputated feet
I drop the kids at day care.
A convergence of emergency vehicles.
The undertaker's heavy sigh.
Mishmash hodgepodge of scallywag.
So long, economy.
Hello, poverty.
The holy aura of lewdness
that unites us.
Making one decision or another
could change—maybe even save—
your life, but most likely won't.
We will never do again what
we didn't half an hour ago.
The difference between a tickle

and blood is inches.
Monster truck bibs and tractor spoons.
Equipment malfunctions
in the language lab. Scandalous
QR codes. The asteroid that destroys
the earth is god. The final gif.
With every word I say
to my kids I wonder how
I'm fucking them up.
There's good drama in that
but what else?
My mother casually informs me
the town where I grew up
is shutting down—
the drug store gone, the post office,
the schools I attended.
What to say about that?
A slow dust devil lifts a sheet
off a strawberry field.
I write this poem while reading this book.
A river rendezvous with its ocean.
I left years ago.

WE USED TO HAVE PARTIES

The city is a kind welcome
of fire   It's on fire
I tell you   not making sense
in the usual sense of the word *sense*
but a meteor's bloom
The bad guys rehearsing
their latest number—
high kicks and all—the good guys watching
videos of unrest in real time
The way you high-fived me
I thought we'd have sex
Such excitement   negates the self
All the cops   standing still
The mask we wear   is assassination
You're cutting out

WE WILL CONTINUE TO SELF-CENSURE

After each page I read I check
how many are left.
A lizard licking its eyes
as I try to remember to forget
how soon you will
forget me. Fear that drives
the anger that drives the fear
that drives the shame.
A frill a minute. Quantum entanglement.
A star without a projector.
Every night until I was 14
I gave my father a bedtime kiss.
Skipped across the pond without
waking the alligators.
Matches are dangerous,
says a kid playing with matches.
The excitement with which we return
home is unwarranted. So I hoard
the language. Drown upside down.
Float like ice. Break some glasses
to break the ice.
I know we're not supposed to sit so much
but fuck it. My colon hurts.
Too many thoughts
begin with "I." The "I"
is immaterial.
If I had my life to live over
I wouldn't.
What a god-awful language.

PRESS ENTER TO EXIT

An interesting development is that I'm about to pass out

My brother has moved to China and I missed
an appointment with the dermatologist to have an unsightly

blemish removed and now am forever
unsightly   A muscle car covered in fallen

lilac petals up higher than the clouds
are high from the ground

A man with a carrot up his sleeve, his arms and legs on fire
is an allusion to an incident involving my father

The difference between having a style and simply repeating
myself is my confusion of late

I misread the word applause as applesauce   My pockets glow

I'm trying very hard   not to be angry

MOUTH FULL OF GROUNDS

The dots are on order   Cops patrol
the larger subway stations
on segways   Nobody
gets out of the way   Yesterday
I had a colonoscopy   which required fasting
for 40 hours and taking so much laxative
I shat water   Now my body is clean
I'm cleansed   and have the opportunity
to put only good things in   To start again
But I can't shake this shadow   I call it death
Love so strong I can hardly
function   Every fight my wife and I have had
or will   Why we can't
love each other like we used to
What will happen   to our children
To date, I'm responsible for the deaths
of at least 20 mice   My most triumphant moment
was when I got 6 at one time on a glue trap
then drowned them in the toilet   At work
we have a meeting in which there is only one rule:
No gerunds   My boss' boss
thinks I'm doing an amazing job
My boss isn't so sure
Blood fills the place on my finger
where I just chewed off some skin
My fear has gone   to waste

REMOVABLE POINTS OF DISCONTINUITY

Very little tells us
we are anything
approaching adequate
Still, I wish you'd fuck me
so we could come   sort of
to an understanding
that from a variety
of external signals
our brains create
things that are not there,
that the words and sentences we believe we hear
are just jumbles of sounds   whistles   grunts   silence
the going energy of content
toward its form

A NEW FORM(ULA)

Plan the future   A presence unknown

             Derivative is the way I hit snooze
for an hour on my alarm each morning

rediscover and marvel at
        my one grey chest hair

When I don't know how to respond
           to people
I don't respond

        This causes obvious problems

Never do I wear
        my sunglasses inside   The (false) modesty

problem forbids me   My low-fat quesadilla
            is especially greasy

The sky sweeps up   the sky

        Brilliance radiates
           from the sun

A crop duster swoops down,
        tips its wings side to side
           as if to say, hi   One day
                      we will all be dead.

I feel best   when I write best

There are many ways I could grow
     my facial hair, but all I do is shave.

         Right now I have no idea how to feel

We want to believe that without love we'd disappear, that if
we have love, give love and know love, we are truly alive and
if there is no love, there would be no life. But the terror is that
without love, life goes on. We go on.

         The soft bullet in
           No mercy
           killing

Your nail polish is the pinkest   of bubble gum

         A ringing endorsement

         My sunglasses are covered in red

         smiley faces

They're There

Lately I have this suspicion
everything sucks.

What some call pressure
I call presence.

The future of the moment.

Ambient break dancing,
            a bowl of bitter beans.

People in general are kind
of stupid and uncaring.

Me included.

Something entirely else is possible,
says the voice in the engineering feedback.

In the shape of a cross in my old
neighborhood are the neon words,
sin will find you out.

When your infant gets a spinal tap
the doctors make you leave the room.

Please, leave the room.

Raising children is boring.
  Sublimely so.

I walk in the door and my mind
  erases.

Things go well, then don't.
  But then, increasingly.

There is never not a narrative.

Little is lonelier
than being married. Except not.

Whatever. Whoever
  you are.

Amputations   all around.

The emperor of hair
does not compare.

I bang my head on something
        then rub it
            as if that will help.

It's my wife's night out.

The kids run
        rough-shod
                over me.

These letters
are my name. My browser
is chrome.

The greatest profit   is destruction.

God's love,
        free parking.

I'll be the sound bite
        if you be the glow.

Lights out for Elmo.

I used to think the way I dressed
meant something.

Now it's just   the way I dress.

I tell my shrink I feel old
        and about my alcoholic friend
        who threatened
        to shoot his wife.

        Give him a hundred dollars.
        Call it a night.

Every time I read
standing on the subway,
people get crushed.

My pen ran out of ink
so I scratched my comments
into the paper,
is a way of saying,
your book destroyed the fuck out of me.

My tie will never enter my pants.
My brand could be your life.

I could handle anything,
      any tragedy that might befall me
if I could be its narrator
      The creator
      Such and so who has left
      the conversation

My feet are cold.

In another room,
my son rolls over.

My daughter sleeps lightly.

It's amazing living in a moment
I have no idea if I'll remember.

My favorite number is six
six six. The first girl I ever fucked

dumped me not long after
the first time we fucked.

The war from before the wars
took over. Blood, accidental.

Such a sad
bastard party.

I never know what it is
I'm taking part in.

When we first met,
my wife thought I was a genius.
She doesn't think that anymore.

We lie together at night.

She sleeps. I watch
amateur porn on my phone.

Then it's all confused robots
and crying dinosaurs.

No safeword necessary.

When we talk
           I feel like
I feel how you want me to   The anatomy
of a skyscraper
           Rubber boots
mistaken for prosthetic legs
                      The loneliness is unbearable

Sometimes I like my own poems
a little too much.

Behold,
my strawberry power. Beware,
my mutilated marginalia. The air

smells like an old sponge.

A daily activity.
Another awesome ending.

I kiss the tiny fingers that hold these shoes.

I generally can't see my head
so when a bird shits there
you can see
how fucked I am.

Prerecorded courtesy.
Repetitive motion death wish
crumpled to a kiss.

A faithful itch.

At times I offend my wife
and do not care.

Others
I'm ashamed.

She breathes into my mouth and I
hold it.

A person in the perfect
disguise of a person.

But love
you are still in love
with me you say

Notes

Poems in this book appropriate material from:

Animal Collective	Email	Meridith's cousin
Atlantic Ocean	Family lore	Not enough women
ATMs	The Flaming Lips	Prince
Ben Hersey	God Speed You! Black Emperor	Radiohead
Bowling	Guitar solos	Rufus Wainwright
The Blood Brothers	Guy next to me on subway	Sampson Starkweather
Bruce Springsteen	Henry Marks	Shirts in windows
Buildings	Jack Spicer	Søren Kierkegaard
Cai Guo-Qiang:	John Keats	Strangers
I Want to Believe	Kid at Costco	Sun Tzu
Charles Olson	Large envelopes	Sylvia Plath
Chris Tonelli	LCD Soundsystem	Talking Heads
Computer errors	Louisa Marks	Ted Berrigan
Coworkers	Lyn Hejinian	These Arms Are Snakes
Dan Boehl	Man chanting on subway platform	Too many dudes
Das Boot	Man at Starbucks	Two Gallants
Dreams	Mary Robison	Tylenol bottles
Elevator buttons	Modest Mouse	*The Wire*
Elisa Gabbert	Meridith Rohana	Wolf Parade

How Do Dinosaurs Say Goodnight?, by Jane Yolen & Mark Teague

"Into the Unforeseen: A Romance of César Aira," by Rivka Galchen, *Harper's Magazine*, June 2011

"The Perfect Game: 5 Years with the Master of Pac-Man," by Joshuah Bearman, *Harper's Magazine*, July 2008

The Sleepy Little Alphabet: A Bedtime Story from Alphabet Town, by Judy Sierra & Melissa Sweet

"Thread by Michael Palmer (New Directions, 2011) and American Fanatics by Dorothy Barresi (Pitt Poetry Series, 2010)," by Jordan Davis, *The Constant Critic*, May 22, 2011

Justin Marks' first book is *A Million in Prizes* (New Issues, 2009), and his latest chapbooks are *We Used to Have Parties* (Dikembe Press, 2014) and *Best Practices* (Greying Ghost, 2013). He is a co-founder of Birds, LLC, an independent poetry press, and lives in Queens, NY with his wife and their twin son and daughter.